The Calvary Code

By

Dr W. E. "Bill" Davies

Note for Librarians: A cataloguing record for this book is available from Library
and Archives Canada at www.collectionscanada.ca/amicus/index-e.html

Printed in Victoria, BC, Canada.

ISBN: 978-1-4251-4251-3 (Soft)
ISBN: 978-1-4251-4252-0 (e-book)

*We at Trafford believe that it is the responsibility of us all, as both individuals
and corporations, to make choices that are environmentally and socially sound.
You, in turn, are supporting this responsible conduct each time you purchase a
Trafford book, or make use of our publishing services. To find out how you are
helping, please visit www.trafford.com/responsiblepublishing.html*

*Our mission is to efficiently provide the world's finest, most comprehensive
book publishing service, enabling every author to experience success.
To find out how to publish your book, your way, and have it available
worldwide, visit us online at www.trafford.com*

Trafford rev. 10/23/2009

 www.trafford.com

North America & international
toll-free: 1 888 232 4444 (USA & Canada)
phone: 250 383 6864 ♦ fax: 812 355 4082 ♦ email: info@trafford.com

This book is dedicated to my good friends in Wales
Roger and Muriel Evans
in appreciation of many hours of sanctified
fellowship, fun and food!

Note: All Scripture passages are taken from The King James Version unless otherwise noted

Introduction

A number of excellent books and tracts have been written, and many equally excellent talks and sermons have been given, combating the message of the Da Vinci Code. Although based on fiction, it has aroused much controversy and speculation. Personally I am convinced that the very best argument against it is the truth about Calvary.

Almost invariably it is the Christian who knows and loves his Lord and his Bible, who knows what Calvary means and what it meant to the Trinity to use Calvary in order to accomplish the Plan of Salvation. The more the believer enters into the meaning of our Lord's sufferings, the more precious He becomes to them. By the same token, the indwelling of the Holy Spirit imparts His own witness to the perfection of the Son of Man, who was also the Son of God.

This means that the Christian is not affected by the Da Vinci Code. As far as he or she is concerned, whatever might be said about Him, whether it is called fact or fiction, has to be tested by Scripture and what the believer knows about the Man of Calvary

In other words, the story of Calvary is quite sufficient. It is heaven's answer to criticism or code!

W E Davies
Cardiff, Wales

Foreword

In its time, the Da Vinci Code, the book and the movie, created a stir within the Christian community. The media also caught the not-so-subtle implications and sensed the furore that was churning among certain sectors of Christianity and attempted as usual to exploit the nervous and the ill-informed. We dealt with the issues involved on radio broadcasts, television, tracts, many books and pamphlets and in the pulpits of many churches across the world. Eventually, the debates diminished, the furore subsided, and, as usual, in these types of flashes-in-the-pan and one-day-wonders, we hardly think about the Da Vinci code any longer.

Of course, this all erupted on the world scene during another of those times when there seems to have been an increase in demonic activity as well. We all sensed yet another planned attack on our faith from various quarters, both serious and uninspired. There was the announcement of the unveiling of The Gospel of Judas and much was made over the "previously undiscovered manuscript". Supposedly revealing another perspective on the early days of the church and offering another "plausible" alternative to the familiar story in the Bible. Many saw this, of course, as a thinly veiled attack on the veracity of the Scriptures and another concentrated manoeuvre by the Enemy to divert our faith and weaken our confidence in the Word of God as the authoritative standard for Life.

This onslaught, too, has faded into memory. Yet, the church carries on. Although continually under siege, scarred and perhaps less than cohesive at times, and not always in harmony in all aspects of a common faith, the Church of the Lord Jesus Christ is alive and well. Over the centuries, numerous songs have been written and many sermons have been preached regarding the repeated attempts to defeat the Church, divide the people of God and minimize or even obliterate our faith in the Scriptures.

For all their recurring attempts and they do not seem to tire of trying again and again whenever they see an opportunity, those who have done so have failed with each attempt. They will continue to fail. You see, God's Word is alive. It is stronger than a two-edged sword. It is a lamp and a light for those of us who believe. It is God's love letter to you and me, sealed in red. It is supernatural and people cannot tolerate that idea in the post modern age.

Amid this continuum of events, Bill Davies has now approached the other fundamental of our faith, the cross of the Lord Jesus and he has done so in a most unusual and appealing manner. Using the backdrop of the Da Vinci Code, he has reached into his extensive storehouse of real life experiences of serving the Lord as a minister of the Gospel for more than 60 years, then using his skill as a poet extraordinaire, he has captured in these pages an anthology of unique poems that look at the cross and the Lamb of God from several distinctive perspectives. That fascinating perspective opens our hearts to see the message of God's love in a exceptional style that only Bill Davies and his poems can provide.

"...the story of Calvary is quite sufficient. It is heaven's answer to criticism or code!" So writes Mr Davies in his Introduction. This sums up this wonderful book of inimitable poems and confirms my feeling that the heart of every person who loves the Lord Jesus will be moved with a new spirit of gratitude after reading this book. I commend it to you.

Greg Sweeting

The Christian Book Shop
Nassau, Bahamas

The Calvary Code

Calvary and the **T**rinity
  reveal a heavenly code

Attracting members of the human **R**ace
  to travel on its road

Love, joy, peace and **I**mmortality
  are Divinely assured

Visions of a world that's **N**ew
  in our lives are stored

As we journey, we are **I**ndwelt
  by our risen Lord

Rejoicing through our trials and **T**ears
  and comforted by His word

Yearning, Lord, to see **Y**ou
  at the end of the Calvary road

Calvary versus Da Vinci

Calvary can never know **D**efeat
it was planned by the Trinity

Ask the angels and the **A**postles
about the Man of Calvary

Listen to Christian **V**oices
across every century

Vast is their spiritual **I**nfluence
confirming Jesus' deity

Acclaimed in Scriptural **N**arrative
is our Lord's virginity

Resist ... vehemently ... **C**hristian
all attacks upon His purity!

Young and old are not **I**mpressed
by the code of Da Vinci

The world ignores Calvary; Satan abhors it – but the Christian adores it.

If we only knew how delighted God is when we say "thank you" to Him for Calvary, we would certainly thank Him more often.

Peter, the Apostle, tells us that the blood of the Lord Jesus is precious(1 Peter 1:18). By comparing 1John 1:7, we get some idea of its preciousness –

- it is the blood of <u>Jesus</u>, which means Saviour;
- it is the blood of <u>Christ</u>, the Messiah of the Jews;
- it is the blood of <u>deity</u> – of the <u>Son of God</u> (His Son);
- it is the blood which <u>cleanses</u>. Notice the continuous tense – it goes on cleansing;
- it is the blood that cleanses <u>from all sin</u>.

"There is wonder working power in the Blood."

There is one thing that we will not want to forget in heaven and the Scriptures clearly reveal that the Trinity does not want us to forget it: Calvary.

Read Revelation Chapter 5.

Calvary is the most important place in the universe. Here are just three reasons –

- the most important **Person** was there
- with a most important **Purpose**
- and the most important **Prayers** were prayed.

See Luke 23:32-33

Facts of Faith

The following facts relate to those who, by faith, have received the Lord Jesus into their lives and praise Him for His work at Calvary

Casting all your care on Him for He careth for you
1 Peter 5:7

All things work together for good for those who love God, And who are called according to His purpose
Romans 8:28

Let not your hearts be troubled
You trust in God, trust also in me
John 14:1

Victory through our Lord Jesus Christ
1 Corinthians 15:57

Able to save to the uttermost all that come to God by Him (the Lord Jesus Christ)
Hebrews 7:25

Resist the devil and he will flee from you
James 4:17

You are my friends,
If you do whatsoever I command you
John 15:14

Christian ...

Brother and Sister,
  millions on earth will never die
  and we'll never have to say goodbye

Assuredly ...

Prophecy makes it very clear
  the Lord's return is very near

Let ...

The Spirit take control
  and pleasing Him be our goal

Victorious ...

Voices fill the air, in joyous expectation
  of our Lord's revelation

Angels

Watching in admiration,
  seeing the church's glorification

Reigning

With our Lord, universally
  we sing triumphantly

You

And I will never say goodbye eternally,
  because of Calvary

Read the last two chapters of Revelation

Calvary – the Miracle Centre of the Universe

The Creator of the universe was **C**rucified
what incomparable humility
Philippians 2:6-8

He was willing to be **A**bandoned
although a member of the Trinity
Psalm 22:1, Matthew 27:46

An earthquake, the sun refused its **L**ight
A criminal found light and liberty
Luke 23:39-45

Many priests saw the rent **V**eil
And turned to Christianity
Acts 6:7

A centurion of the Roman **A**rmy
recognised Deity
Matthew 27:54

Folded clothes, an empty tomb ... **R**esurrection
Saints returning from eternity
Matthew 27:54, Mark 16:6

Jesus ... Christ ... Messiah ... **Y**ahweh
Controller and Lord of history
Exodus 3:14, 6:3, Matthew 28:19-20,
Philippians 2:9-11, Hebrews 13:8

Unlocking the Mystery of Jesus' work on Calvary

Covering
> God shed the blood of an animal to clothe Adam and Eve after they had sinned and discovered their nakedness before God. It speaks of the death of the Lord Jesus so that we might be clothed with righteousness
>> *Genesis 3:21, Isaiah 61:10, 2Corinthians 5:21*

Abraham and Isaac
> The story of Abraham and Isaac is a wonderfully prophetic profile of Calvary
>> *Genesis 22, John 3:16*

Lamb of God
> Jesus is the Lamb of God; He is also the Passover Lamb
>> *Read Exodus 12, John 1:29 and 1 Corinthians 5:7*

Veil of the Temple
> The veil within the Temple represents the flesh (the body) of our Lord Jesus
> *Read what happened to the veil when Jesus died in*
>> *Matthew 27:51*
>> *And see its meaning in Hebrews 10:20*

Ark of the Covenant

The Ark is a beautiful type of the Lord. The contents speak of Him. It had a "mercy seat". Once a year the High Priest sprinkled it with blood and atoned for the sins of the nation for the year ahead

Exodus 30:15-16, Romans 5:11

Resurrection and the Life

This is a unique title of our Lord. This claim would not have any validity for the death on the Cross if He had not risen.

Psalm 16:10-11, Isaiah 53:10-11, John 11:25

Yom Kippur

This sums up all that has been stated above – see especially the section on the Resurrection and the Life. Yom Kippur refers to the Day of Atonement and was celebrated once a year. However, atonement did not become absolute until the Son of God completed the plan of salvation at Calvary

Read prayerfully John 19:30 and Hebrews 9:26

Prophecies

It has been claimed that about one third of the Bible is devoted to prophecies written hundreds of years before the events they foretold. Over three hundred of these prophecies concerned the coming of the Messiah, whose virgin birth, tribe, family, place of birth, redeeming death, burial, resurrection, ascension and second coming were all predicted in the Old Testament, which itself was completed by 450 BC.

As Mary, the mother of Jesus, stood with the others at Calvary, she might well have recalled the prophecy which she heard from Simeon thirty three years earlier:

"Yea, a sword shall pierce through thy own soul also..." (Luke 2:35)

Mary's heart broke as she personally experienced the fulfilment of Simeon's prophecy. She would also recall pronouncements of Old Testament prophets like Isaiah who, seven centuries before, had described in detail the sufferings to be endured by the Messiah:

"He is despised and rejected of men; a man of sorrows, and acquainted with grief: and we hid, as it were, our faces from Him; He was despised, and we esteemed Him not. Surely He has borne our griefs, and carried our sorrows: yet we ourselves esteemed Him stricken, smitten of God, and afflicted. But He was wounded for our transgressions, He was bruised for our iniquities: the chastisement of our peace was upon Him; and with His stripes we are healed" (Isaiah 53:3-5)

Prophecies concerning the vicarious death of the Messiah upon the cross were superfluous at Calvary: It was there that predictions gave place to fulfilment.

The Christian can shout, *"Hallelujah"* because *"those things which God before had shewed by the mouth of all His prophets, that Christ should suffer, HE HATH SO FULFILLED"* (Acts 3:18)ˑ

Taken from "Missing at Calvary" also written by
Bill Davies

Pilate's wife was very upset. She had had a bad dream. It was during the day. Had it been at night, it could have been called a nightmare.

We are not told what was in the dream, but she was so upset that she sent a message to her husband advising him to *"have nothing to do with this just Man, for I have suffered many things this day because of Him."*

There have been several suggestions about the nature of her dream. One of the most dramatic is that she saw the Lord Jesus standing before her husband being judged by him. Then, in her dream, the scene changed, her husband was then being judged, *"by Him who sits on a throne."*

Her dream must have been a very real and frightening experience.

Maybe *"that just Man"* was sitting on *"a Great White Throne"* and His eyes were filled with holy anger. Perhaps we shall know one day. One thing is sure – she will know who *"that just Man"* is in that hour. She will know, too, perhaps she did know, that her husband, although very reluctantly, had taken part in the crucifixion of the Jewish Messiah who was the Son of God – her Creator.

Read the whole of Matthew 27

A friend gave me a rather unusual quotation some time ago. You might like to know it: "It *is said that 20:20 hindsight is the perfect science."*

This may be true of humans but it cannot apply to God. He lives in an ever present NOW. He doesn't need hindsight. That's why we are told *"He (the Lord Jesus) was the Lamb slain from the foundation of the world."* By the same token He knew all about you and me before we were born.

See Revelation 13:8

A Calvary Creed

I believe that -

The Lord Jesus Christ is our **C**reator
John 1:10, 1 Timothy 3:16

Jesus was a sinless man and God **A**lmighty
Isaiah 9:6-8, Matthew 1:21,23

He is the personification of Divine **L**ove
John 3:16, Romans 5:5-7, 1 John 4:8

Born and subject to the **V**irgin
Luke 2:51-52, John 2:1-5

Suffered for our sins, arose and **A**scended
Matthew 27, Luke 24, Acts 1

Glorified in heaven, soon to **R**eturn
John 14:1-3, Revelation 19:16;20:4

Then to reign throughout the eternal **Y**ears
Isaiah 9:7, Luke 1:33

The Sun

"And it was about the sixth hour, and there was a darkness over all the earth until the ninth hour. And the sun was darkened..."

(Luke 23:44-45)

On the first Good Friday, after man had done his worst in perpetrating the cruellest of tortures and ignominy upon the Son of God, Jesus endured for three hours God's judgement for the sins of the whole world – your sins and mine. Is it any wonder that Jesus, when He had suffered at the hand of God the punishment deserved by the whole of mankind, cried out, *"My God, my God, why hast thou forsaken me?"* It is also significant that during this suffering - between noon and three o'clock – there was darkness over the land.

It has been conjectured that the darkness was due to one of the occasional eclipses of the sun, but this could not be. On that Good Friday the respective positions of the sun and the moon made an eclipse of the sun astronomically impossible.

The absence of light could have been a symbol of the darkness that overtook the sinless Son of God as He suffered on the cross. Or was the darkness an intervention by God to veil His Son from the gaze of men, as Jesus, who knew no sin, suffered for the sins of the whole world?

Whatever the significance of the absence of the light, every believer can rejoice that because of what took place during those three hours of darkness, the light of the gospel has illuminated their lives like no other incandescence. *"For God, who commanded the light to shine out of darkness, hath shined in our hearts, to give the light of the knowledge of the glory of God in the face of Jesus Christ"* (2 Corinthians 4:6)

Taken from "Missing at Calvary" also written by Bill Davies

Calvary cancels it all

Calvary cancels it all
  every sinful thought

All unrighteous actions
  and idols we have sought

Liberating minds
  from errors we've been taught

Visions of fame and fortune
  thankfully come to naught

All to Jesus we belong
  by Calvary we've been bought

Redeemed by His precious blood
  and by His Spirit taught

You and I willingly
  by Calvary's wonder have been caught

May I suggest that you read the accounts of Calvary in the Gospels?

What, I wonder, were the emotions of angels and humans at Calvary? They were almost certainly varied and mixed. Angels were not allowed beyond Gethsemane. One of them strengthened our Lord in the garden – but so far and no further. How many people among the crowd had been healed by Him, had seen Him perform miracles, and heard Him speak?

It may be possible in heaven to get angelic and human reactions to Calvary, one day.
See 1 Peter 1:12 and Luke 23:48

Surely, one of the greatest wonders in heaven will be our ability to actually see the human face of God with the marks of Calvary still on it.
See Psalm 71:7

The Calvary Code affects our:

Characters   as   **C**hristians

<u>OUTWARDLY</u>

Attitudes   and   **A**ppetites

<u>SPIRITUALLY</u>

Lives   and   **L**oves

<u>INWARDLY</u>

Values   and   **V**iewpoints

<u>SOCIALLY</u>

Affections   and   **A**gonies

<u>PHYSICALLY</u>

Reasonings   and   **R**egrets

<u>PROBLEMATICALLY</u>

Yearning for eternal **Y**outh

<u>UNDERSTANDABLY</u>

Because our Lord yielded His body to His death at Calvary, God revealed, by His Spirit, that this was His *"good and acceptable and perfect will"* and fully ratified by the other two members of the Trinity.

Romans 12:1-3

In a billion years' time, Calvary and the wonderful work of redemption, procured for us by our precious Lord, will still be uppermost in our mind. Shall we sing some of the lovely hymns from planet earth, such as "When I survey the wondrous cross"? Or Charles Wesley's hymn "And can it be"? And can we possibly imagine heaven without Handel's Messiah or Fanny Crosby's wonderful hymns?

Perhaps we shall compose our own, based on our personal experience of the Lord and what He did for us at Calvary.

Read Revelation 5

Had I a thousand gifts beside,
I'd cleave to Jesus crucified
And build on Him alone;
For no foundation there is given
On which I'd place my hopes of heaven
But Christ the corner-stone

Old hymn

Angels

The Bible records that throughout history angels played a major role in implementing God's plan for the world, revealing God's will, executing His judgement and providing protection for God's people. Jesus, at the conclusion of telling the story of the lost piece of silver, told His hearers, *"Likewise I say to you, there is joy in the presence of the angels of God over one sinner that repents"* (Luke 15:10). Jesus said, *"Whosoever shall confess me before men, him shall the Son of Man also confess before the angels of God...."* (Luke 12:8). Of angels the writer of the Epistle to the Hebrews says in chapter 1 verse 14 *"Are they not all ministering spirits, sent forth to minister for them who shall be heirs of salvation?"*

Angels were active in the life of Jesus. Angels announced His birth; angels, after Jesus had triumphed over the severe test of the devil in the wilderness, came and ministered to Him (Matthew 4:11); an angel visited the garden of Gethsemane to strengthen Him before He went to Calvary; angels were at the tomb after the resurrection, when one proclaimed, *"He is not here – He is risen"*; angels were probably present at His ascension; and ten thousand angels will accompany Him at His second coming.

But there were no angels at Calvary. Gethsemane, it seems, was the boundary at which God drew a line and beyond which angels could not go. There was to be no help for Jesus at Calvary – either human or angelic. The angels could only look on from a distance, perplexed and mystified as God's great eternal plan of salvation unfolded and the eternal Son of God suffered for the sins of the world. Jesus could have called for twelve legions of angels to come to His aid, but He had to fulfil God's plan of salvation alone.

There were no angels at Calvary – it was *"BY HIMSELF He purged our sins."* (Hebrews 1:3)

Who was crucified at Calvary?

Creator....the Almighty God
John 1:10, 1 Timothy 3:16

Ancient of days
Daniel 7:22

Lion of the tribe of Judah
Revelation 5:5

Virgin born .... Son of God
Isaiah 9:6, Matthew 1:23

Alpha and Omega
Revelation 1:8

Ruler in Israel
Micah 5:2

Yahweh ... Jehovah ... Jesus
Exodus 3:14, Matthew 1:23

An Altar

Most of those who stood around the cross needed no reminder of the importance of the altar in their nation's history. Abraham, Jacob and Moses – to mention only a few – built their altars in worship to God. The children of Israel had their altars in the tabernacle as they journeyed through the wilderness and in the temple when they settled in the land to which God led them.

At the time of the crucifixion, the altar still had a major role in the religious ritual of the Jews. Daily the people brought their animal sacrifices, and by laying their hands on them before they were killed identified themselves with their offering. The people were aware of the significance of these offerings, for God had told Moses, *"It is the blood that maketh atonement for the soul"* (Leviticus 17:11)

The Jewish historian Josephus records that, at the Passover feast in Jerusalem, about 250,000 offerings were made by the people. Sadly, most of the offerers failed to recognise that the many sacrifices offered foreshadowed the one sacrifice of the spotless Lamb of God who would bear away the sins of the whole world. *"Without the shedding of blood is no remission"* (Hebrews 9:22)

During the crucifixion the temple worship continued as usual. That day, at the ninth hour – 3.00pm – when the evening sacrifice was being offered, Jesus cried with a loud voice, *"It is finished"*. The Messiah had finished His work, and consequently the altars and the offerings were no longer necessary. Millions of sacrifices had been offered on many altars down through the centuries, but Calvary had now made them unnecessary.

"Once at the end of the age hath He appeared to put away sin by the sacrifice of Himself" (Hebrews 9:26)

Taken from "Missing at Calvary" also written by Bill Davies

You are bought with a price

1 Corinthians 6:20

You are bought by **C**hrist
You are not your own

The price He paid was **A**bsolute
It can never be known

The reason was His **L**ove
And His will to atone

The divine and eternal **V**ision
Compelled Him to leave His throne

Suffering ... Dying ... **A**bandoned
He endured the cost alone

Has He become your **R**edeemer?
Have you heard His pleasing tone?

Thank Him, He will hear **Y**ou
Then your destiny is known

Beauty

Prophesying Messiah's utterances seven centuries before Calvary, Isaiah wrote, *"I gave my back to the smiters, and my cheeks to them that plucked off the hair: I hid not my face from shame and spitting"* and *"He hath no form or comeliness; and when we shall see Him, there is no beauty that we should desire Him"*

(Isaiah 50:6 and 53:2)

The followers of Jesus had daily looked on His holy face. They had seen His determination when, knowing what awaited Him there, *"He steadfastly set His face to go to Jerusalem."* (Luke 9:51). Peter, James and John, when Jesus took them up into a high mountain, saw His face shining as the sun. (Matthew 17:2)

Among those standing around the cross were probably some who had come face to face with Jesus: people like Zaccheus and Bartimeus. Bartimeus, whose sight Jesus restored and who, as long as he lived, would not forget the first time he saw the face of Jesus as he was able to see for the first time.

But that beautiful face was now *"marred more than any man, and His form more than the sons of men"* (Isaiah 52:14). Before they led Jesus to Calvary, *"they spit in His face, and buffeted Him; and others smote Him with the palms of their hands.*" (Matthew 26:67). All this – and more – He endured for you and me.

For the Christian it will be wonderful to see their believing loved ones who preceded them to heaven; but the greatest experience for all believers, when they are present with their Lord, will be the fulfilment of the prophecy of Isaiah: *"thine eyes shall see the King in His beauty"* (Isaiah 33:17)

Taken from "Missing at Calvary" also written by
Bill Davies

A Physician

Crucifixion was a form of capital punishment imposed by many nations including the Romans, whose emperor, Constantine I, abolished it in the 4th century AD.

In those countries where capital punishment is extant, a physician is invariably present to certify death; but there was no physician for this task at Calvary. Indeed, the Romans left the crucified victims to die for many days, and left the bodies for the dogs and the vultures to devour.

The Jewish law required that if a man committed a sin worthy of death, and he should be put to death by hanging on a tree, his body should not remain all night on the tree, but should be buried on the day of execution (Deuteronomy 21:22,23). The Mishnah – a collection of exegetical material written about 200 AD – laid down *"Everyone who allows the dead to remain overnight transgresses a positive command."*

It was even more vital that on that particular Friday bodies should not remain on the crosses after 6pm when the Sabbath – the Passover Sabbath – commenced. To accelerate death at Calvary, the soldiers broke the legs of the malefactors, but when they saw that Jesus was already dead they did not break His legs.

This decision, not to break the legs of Jesus, must have struck the consciences of those Jews who knew their Scriptures. In a few hours the Passover supper would be eaten. There would be the slain lamb, for whom the Scriptures directed that not a bone of it should be broken (Numbers 9:12). They may also have recalled David's Messianic prophecy, *"He keepeth all His bones: not one of them is broken."* (Psalm 34:20).

There was no human physician to tend to the suffering Saviour at Calvary. But the great Physician, who healed many when on earth, continues His ministry today, healing bodies and souls.

Taken from "Missing at Calvary" also written by Bill Davies

The fruit of Calvary

When the seed of faith is sown in the soil of Calvary
Some of the results are as follows:

Human   lives   are   **C**hanged
2 Corinthians 5:17

Many spiritual questions are **A**nswered
1 Corinthians 15

Lives   overflow   with   **L**ove
Romans 5:5

An appreciation of Christian **V**alues begins
Matthew 5:3-16

A conviction of   Scriptural **A**uthority enters
2 Timothy 3:16

An expectation of the Lord's **R**eturn convicts
Titus 2:13

Also His presence over the **Y**ears is assured
Matthew 28:20

Easter Morn

"Now upon the first day of the week, very early in the morning, they came unto the sepulchre... and they found the stone rolled away from the sepulchre. And they entered in, and found not the body of the Lord Jesus"
Luke 24:1-3

Shades of night steal away,
Birds their chorus singing;
The grass is wet,
The Garden still;
Hark! A woman weeping.

A moment past describing,
A day of days is this –
His voice, her name, His presence,
The memory will not fade,
This is eternal bliss.

Angels vigil keeping,
The stone, the seal are gone;
God is in His Garden –
Away with sorrow's weeping,
This is Easter Morn!

Taken from "Missing at Calvary" also written by
Bill Davies

Why not read the wonderful story through in the Gospels?
And then finish by reading 1 Corinthians chapter 15.

Not only did the writers of the four gospels record the resurrection of Jesus but so did historians. One of these was Josephus who was born AD 37, the year that Caligula acceded to the throne of the Roman Empire. Josephus therefore lived during the years when many who saw Jesus after His resurrection were still alive.

For many years Josephus was a Jewish priest. He was no advocate for Christianity, yet he wrote of Jesus:

'Now there was about this time, Jesus, a wise man, if it be legal to call him a man, for he was a doer of wonderful works – a teacher of such men as receive the truth with pleasure. He drew over to him both many of the Jews and many of the Gentiles. He was Christ; and when Pilate, at the suggestion of the principal men amongst us, had condemned him to the cross, those that loved him at the first did not forsake him, for he appeared to them alive again the third day, as the divine prophets had foretold these and ten thousand other wonderful things concerning him; and the tribes of Christians, so named from him, are not extinct at this day'

(Antiquities of the Jews, Chapter 3 from the COMPLETE WORKS OF FLAVIUS JOSEPHUS - a combination of the William Whiston translation published by William P Nimmo, Edinburgh, Scotland in 1867 and the Standard Edition published by Porter and Coates, Philadelphia, USA. Published by Kregel Publications, Grand Rapids, Michigan, USA)

Many have attempted to disprove the resurrection of Jesus but their research has caused them to conclude that the evidence for the resurrection was irrefutable. One of these was Frank Morison, a lawyer, who in his book *'Who moved the Stone'* wrote that he was brought up in a rationalistic environment, and had come to opinion that the resurrection was nothing but a fairy tale happy ending which spoiled the matchless story of Jesus. He therefore planned to write an account of the last tragic days of Jesus, allowing the full horror of the crime and the full heroism of Jesus to shine through, but would exclude any suspicion of the miraculous and utterly discount the resurrection. But Morison later admitted that when he studied the facts with care, he had to change his mind, and he did write his book in which he cited the most convincing evidence in support of the resurrection.

Upon the cross at Calvary, Jesus bore the sins of the world – including every reader of these pages. But He did not remain on the cross. He rose again and by His Holy Spirit dwells in the hearts of all who put their faith in Him as their personal Saviour.

The Risen Lord

"Now in the place where He was crucified there was a garden; and in the garden a new sepulchre, wherein was never man yet laid" (John 19:41)

These words recorded by the apostle John make it clear that Calvary was not only the place where Jesus was crucified but it was also the place where He was buried. It was, therefore, also from Calvary that Jesus rose from the tomb and which led to the proclamation of the angel to the women *"He is not here; for He is risen, as He said"*. (Matthew 28:6)

Shortly before Jesus died at Calvary, He cried, *"It is finished"*, (John 19:30) a statement which in Greek is one word 'tetelstai'. This meant that Jesus had reached the end of His sufferings. It was a note of triumph – spoken in a loud voice – which proclaimed a mighty victory won. Indeed, it is the same word as the apostle John used when he wrote, *"...Jesus, knowing that all things were now <u>accomplished</u>..."* (John 19:28).

The language of Wales – one of the ancient Brythonic Celtic languages – grew from the language spoken by the Britons at the time of the Roman invasion. It is still spoken by about one fifth of Wales' 3 million population. The publication of a Bible in Welsh, in 1536, made a major contribution to keeping the language alive. In Welsh there are two words for finished. One is *'diwedd'* which can be seen on road signs in the Principality to notify drivers when they have come to the end of road works. The same word is used in television schedules to describe the end of a programme and the end of the transmissions for the day. Significantly, the translators did not use *'diwedd'* for Jesus' word *'finished'*. Instead they used *'Gorffennwyd'* which means not the end but the *'completion, accomplished, achieved, done'*. For Jesus the cross was not the end; it was the perfect fulfilment of His mission to die for the sins of mankind on the cross which was followed by His physical resurrection.

Many Infallible Proofs in Scripture

Acts 1:3

Come and see the place where the Lord lay
Matthew 28:6

All Hail (said the Lord Jesus)
And they came and held Him by His feet
Matthew 28:9

Lord, wilt Thou at this time
Restore again the kingdom to Israel?
Acts 1:6

Victory that overcomes the world
Even our faith
1 John 5:4

And Thomas answered Him
My Lord and my God
John 20:28

Rejected of men
Isaiah 53:3

You disowned the holy and righteous One
And asked for a murderer to be granted to you
Acts 3:14

HEAVEN

Because of all that our Lord did for us at Calvary, heaven will be free of many things. Note some of them.

Conflict.   Isaiah's prophecy, which can be read on the United Nations building in New York, will come true.

Isaiah 2:4

Afflictions.   We shall enjoy perfect health. The Scriptures teach that we shall eat and drink in the Kingdom. It will be perfect food absorbed in perfect bodies. It will be eternal freedom from aging and sickness.

Matthew 26:29, Luke 24:41-43

Losers.   No losers in heaven. All winners in and through the finished work of redemption.

Revelation 5

Visions.   No need for visions in heaven. It is a place of absolute reality. A place of sublime simplicity and simply sublime!

John 14:1-3, Revelation 21:7

Abandonment.   Humans, many of them children have known this terrible experience on earth. But in heaven - never again!

Hebrews 13:5

Regeneration.   When we are *'born again'* on earth, we shall never need to be born again in heaven

John 3:3

Years.   Time with its divisions will end. It will be a timeless, triumphant and thankful day that will never end. Hallelujah!

John 3:16, Revelation 22:1-5

A Reward

As a boy I remembered my father buying each week the "John Bull" magazine, which included a competition called "Bullets." A clue, or a *bullet*, was provided and readers were invited to write a pithy and imaginative phrase which amplified the *bullet*. One week the *bullet* was "For services rendered," and a few weeks later the magazine printed the winning entry, *"For services rendered – pinned on a Cross"*

I was much impressed with the brilliance of the implied double meaning; the first a reminder of the brave who for services rendered in the First World War had been decorated with the Military Cross; but the second meaning, although less obvious, was more profound. The Saviour, in laying down His life for the whole of humanity, rendered incalculable services but He received no public acclamation or reward. On the contrary, He was pinned on a cross.

But recognition for Jesus will come. Describing this, the apostle Paul declared, *"and being found in fashion as a man, He humbled Himself, and became obedient unto death, even the death of the cross. Wherefore God also has highly exalted Him and given Him a name that is above every name: that at the name of Jesus every knee should bow, of things in heaven and on earth and under the earth; and that every tongue should confess that Jesus Christ is Lord to the glory of God the Father"* *Philippians 2:8-11*

There was no reward at Calvary for Jesus, but His resurrection on the third day and His exaltation into God's right hand were His immediate reward. Then, in a coming day, when every tongue confesses that Jesus is Lord, His reward will be complete.

Taken from "Missing at Calvary" also written by
Bill Davies

Blessings flow from Calvary

"Blessed with all spiritual blessings" – Ephesians 1:3

We know the indwelling of **C**hrist
Galatians 2:20

We experience the ministry of **A**ngels
Hebrews 1:14

We enjoy divine love and eternal **L**ife
John 3:16, Romans 5:5

We've seen a special spiritual **V**ision
Hebrews 2:9

Available to us is God's **A**rmour
Ephesians 6:13-18

We're heirs to God's glorious **R**iches
Ephesians 1:7, 3:16

We've the expectation of eternal **Y**outh
Psalm 103:1-5, Revelation 21:4

Wonderful Benefits of Calvary

Complete deliverance of **C**reation
Romans 8:20-21

God has become **A**pproachable
John 3:16, 14:6

Christians enjoy spiritual **L**iberty
John 8:36

Appreciation of heaven's **V**alues
Matthew 5:2-12

Experiencing the ministry of **A**ngels
Hebrews1:14

Clothed in Christ's **R**ighteousness
2 Corinthians 5:21

Satisfying a desire for eternal **Y**outhfulness
Psalm 103:5-6

A Royal Crown

There was no royal crown for the suffering Saviour at Calvary. No *diadema*, (the kingly crown worn by kings of Persia, Alexander the Great and Roman Emperors) was placed on the head of the King of Kings at Calvary. Instead, a mock crown of thorns adorned His head as He hung upon the cross.

Those thorns were evidence of the curse that came upon all nature when man sinned in the Garden of Eden (Genesis 3:17-19). In another garden, Calvary, (John 19:41), the King of Kings who knew no sin was *"made sin for us"* (2 Corinthians 5:21). And *"redeemed us from the curse of the law by becoming a curse for us"* (Galatians 3:13). That crown of thorns was a symbol of the burden that Jesus bore for you and me.

No crown for Jesus at Calvary, but because He bore the curse there and rose again, *"we see Jesus, who was made a little lower than the angels for the suffering of death, crowned with glory and honour"* (Hebrews 2:9). *"For He is Lord of Lords, and King of Kings; and they that are with Him are called, and chosen and faithful."* (Revelation 17:14).

No royal crown for the Saviour at Calvary: but, to the apostle Paul the believers at Thessalonica were *"his crown of rejoicing"* (1 Thessalonians 2:19). For those in His kingdom, through personal faith in Him, in a day coming there is a crown of righteousness (2 Timothy 4:8), an incorruptible crown (1 Corinthians 9:24,25), a crown of life (James 1:12), and a crown of glory that fadeth not away (1Peter 5:4)

Taken from "Missing at Calvary" also written by Bill Davies

Singing

From early days singing and dancing were important in Jewish religion. In *the temple "four thousand praised the Lord with instruments"* (1 Chronicles 23:5), and *"two hundred fourscore and eight were instructed in the songs of the Lord"* (1 Chronicles 25:7). Singing was part of the liturgy in the synagogues of Jesus' day.

The Passover, celebrated by Jesus and the twelve before Calvary, concluded with singing; *"and when they had sung a hymn, they went out into the Mount of Olives."* (Matthew 26:30). It is impossible to enter into the emotions of Jesus as He sang that hymn – the Hallel, Psalms 113 to 118 – which include the words *"God is the Lord, which hath shewed us light: bind the sacrifice with cords, even unto the horns of the altar"* (Psalm 118:27). But there was no singing at Calvary.

The Apostle John records the scene in heaven after the death, resurrection and ascension of Jesus, *"and I beheld, and, lo, in the midst of the throne...stood a Lamb as it had been slain... and they sung a new song, saying, 'thou art worthy to take the book, and to open the seals thereof; for Thou wast slain, and hast redeemed us to God by Thy blood out of every kindred, and tongue, and people, and nation'"* (Revelation 5:6,9)

No singing at Calvary, but because of what took place there, throughout the world people of many tribes, nations and denominations sing from their hearts hymns of praise of the One who died there.

No singing at Calvary, but because of Calvary praise on earth now, and in heaven, throughout eternity

Taken from "Missing at Calvary" also written by
Bill Davies

Calvary from Scripture and Hymns

The following words are from our inspired Scriptures and Christian hymns. They have a deep spiritual meaning for the Christian in light of Calvary

Cleanses from all sin

1 John1:7

And can it be that I should gain
      An interest in the Saviour's blood?
      Died He for me who caused His pain?
      For me – who Him to death pursued?
Charles Wesley

Lord, you know everything. You know that I love You
John 21:17

Verily, there is a reward for the righteous
PSALM 58:11, 1 Corinthians 1:30

As for me and my house, we will serve the Lord
Joshua 24:15

Rock of Ages, cleft for me
      Let me hide myself in Thee
Augustus M Toplady

You are my friends if you do whatever I command you
John 15:14

The church that has the Lord Jesus at the centre of its worship, and keeps Calvary before it as a remembrance of His death and resurrection, will rarely, if ever, know modernism or anything of a worldly nature.

See Matthew 18:20

Dr. Luke in his gospel mentions *"the place called Calvary"* (Luke 23:33). It is the only place in the Bible where the word "Calvary" is mentioned. The other gospels call it *"the place of the skull"* which is the Hebrew for the same place. The following simple acrostic may help you, in a small way, to understand a little more of this wonderful place.

Place of **P**ower	John 10:17-18
Place of **L**ove	John 3:16, Galatians 2:20
Place of **A**bandonment	Matthew 27:46
Place of **C**ommitment	Hebrews 10:7-10
Place of **E**quality	Romans 3:23,1 Timothy 3:16

The Apostle Paul wrote to the church at Rome and beseeched them to *"present (yield) their bodies as a living sacrifice to God."* He said that this was an *"act of intelligent worship."* In the context, Paul makes it clear that the Christian should do so, in view of *"the mercies of God."* One of the greatest of these mercies was the accomplishment of the work of redemption at Calvary. A prayerful reading of the previous chapters will confirm this, especially chapters 1-8 of this letter to the church at Rome.

Romans 12:1-2

Calvary's message for Christians

"You are not your own, you are bought with a price"
1 Corinthians 6:19-20

Christian, you do not belong to you
I do not belong to me

All things are new, eternally
because of Calvary

Life can never be the same
daily or personally

Values are now absolute
we cling to them cheerfully

Also our spirit, soul and body are His
paradoxically, we yield them daily

Resurrection life becomes a blessing
with the help of the Trinity

You and I will never belong to you and me.
because we are His, eternally

The A.B.C Road to and from
CALVARY

A is for ATONEMENT - planned eternally.
Revelation 13:8

B When we think of Calvary
We think of His BLOOD – shed vicariously.
1 John 1:7

C The Church will never forget His loving COMMITMENT
to His spiritual, mental and physical agony.
Revelation 5

D This reminds us that God cannot DIE, but the man
who died was a member of the Trinity.
John 1:10, 3:16 and 1 Timothy 3:16

E He claimed EQUALITY with the Father, and God
confirmed it – publicly.
Matthew 17:5, John 14:6-10, 14

F This word is FAITH and it reminds us that along the
road of life, to obtain forgiveness and salvation, it is
an absolute necessity.
John 3:16, Romans10:9

G This leads us to the garden, where He sweat drops of blood – GETHSEMANE.

Matthew 26:46-56

H HEAVEN is the word. It is hope for the Christian and a place of eternal security.

John 10:28-29, 14:1-3

I This big, little word, leads us to one of the most used titles of our Lord Jesus. It speaks of His deity. It is *"I AM"*. We call Him *"the second person of the Trinity."*

John 8:58

J We can't write this letter without remembering JESUS. It tells us of His earthly ministry and humility.

Matthew 1:23,25

K The Apostle Peter tells us that we are *"KEPT by the power of God through faith .."* This is the experience of the Christian daily and continuously.

1 Peter 1:5

L What a lovely word LOVE is. At the precise moment we yield to His control He *"sheds it abroad in our hearts by the Holy Spirit"* – freely and abundantly.

Romans 5:5

M When you saw the letter M, did you think of MARY, the mother of our Lord? When she said, *"all generations will call me blessed"* did she have an idea that she would be the most blessed human being in all history, or was she speaking prophetically?

Luke 1:48

N This letter leads us to NAZARETH, where our Creator lived for thirty years with a human family.

Luke 2:51

O OMNIPOTENT is a good, theological word that describes the Lord even during His visit to earth. All powerful, 100% deity and 100% perfect humanity.

John 10:17-18

P Would you choose the word PRAYER for our letter here? I think you would if you knew that, almost certainty, the greatest prayers were prayed at Calvary. They are the prayers of the deity for the salvation of humanity. Probably the greatest is *"My God, my God, why have you forsaken me?"* Probably the greatest prayer in divine and human history?

Matthew 27:22

Q QUESTION? Which is the most important question a human being can ask himself? Pontius Pilate, in the shadow of Calvary, asked himself that very question. It decides our destiny.   Read His question in Matthew 27:22

Matthew 27:46

R The reason for the choice of the word RISEN will be easily understood by the believer. *"He is risen"* are probably the three greatest words in the angelic vocabulary.

Mark 16:6

S As we draw to the end of the A.B.C Road we notice the word STRANGER. Two people walking on another road met Him. They had seen Him previously, many times. Now, He was a stranger to them. I wonder why! At the end of their journey, suddenly, they knew Him! They were sure of His identity and dashed back to Jerusalem to tell the disciples. Read about it. It is a wonderful story!

Luke 24

T Mary Magdalene, when she knew who it was, held Him, and He said to her *"TOUCH me not for I am not yet ascended to my Father.."* She would remember that wonderful day. His lovely voice calling her name, gently telling her not to touch Him and giving the reason, etc. In heaven she still remembers that wonderful morning. What better memory for all eternity?

John 20:17

U Can you think of a better word than the word UNIQUE? I'm thinking of the word in John 3:16 in the French Bible *"...He gave His UNIQUE Son..."* Calvary, the Christian the Church and all creation prove this – uniquely!

V Some students of the prophetic Scriptures believe that Psalm 22, which is a Messianic Psalm, teaches, in verse 22, that the Lord Jesus will sing a solo in the midst of the Church in heaven. This seems to be confirmed in Hebrews 2:12. We have, therefore, the word VOICE suggested by the letter V. If He is going to sing to the Church, what might He sing? Probably a hymn about Calvary!

Compare Revelation 5

W W stands for WORSHIP. If Calvary hadn't happened, there would be no Church and no Christian on earth or in heaven. We almost certainly would not worship Him in hell. Soon we shall discover the meaning, as never before, of the privilege and blessing of worship in eternity!

John 4:21-24

X You might think it is difficult to find an X word in relation to the Lord Jesus and/or Calvary. Actually it is one of the best on our A.B.C Road. The dictionary says "as an abbreviation it represents the word Christ in Christmas - Xmas". We say thank you Lord for your advent at Bethlehem. Without it there would have been no Calvary Code or Calvary journey.

Isaiah 53, John 1:1, 1 Timothy 3:16

Y As we approach the end of our journey, would you allow me to be a little personal and use the word YOU? May I very tenderly say "if you are not a Christian, YOU must be born again" and "if you are a Christian are you totally surrendered to the control of the Holy Spirit and to the Man of Calvary?"

John 3:3,7, Romans 12;1-2, Galatians 5:18
Ephesians 5:18

Z As we end our journey, having stopped at 25 sign posts on the way, there is one that finalises it – it sums it all up. It is the best in my dictionary and it is found in Scripture which wonderfully confirms it. It is the word ZEAL. It is so important that we must quote the words of the Psalm, *"The zeal of Thy house has consumed me"* - note that this Psalm is Messianic and the Lord Jesus is speaking prophetically.

Psalm 69:9

CLOSING THOUGHTS

Rudyard Kipling once wrote

> *I have six faithful serving men*
> *Who taught me all I knew*
> *Their names are*
> *What and Where and When*
> *And How and Why and Who*

At the end of this book let's use these six *'men'* to draw us to Calvary. Let's give thanks to our Lord for His wonderful love for us. Let's again remember that wonderful place called Calvary.

What shall I do with Jesus?
Matthew 27:22

Where I record My name I will come to you and bless you
Exodus 20:24

When they came to the place called Calvary, there they crucified Him.
Luke 23:33

How shall we escape if we neglect so great salvation?

Hebrews 2:3

Why do you seek the living among the dead? He is not here - He is risen!

Luke 24:5-6

Who are you Lord? I am Jesus whom you are persecuting

Acts 9:5

You may be interested in these other publications by W. E. Davies:

Fifty-Two Echoes of Calvary

A weekly devotional book centred on Calvary. The reader may meditate on the wonder of Calvary using this book to help focus the heart on Golgotha and the crucified Son of God who died there for the sins of the human race.

The Miracle Prayer

A small booklet that explains the wonderful outcome for praying the Miracle Prayer. Beginning with an explanation of what the Miracle Prayer is, Mr Davies gives many illustrations and practical results that come from a sincere person who prays this prayer.

Bible Quiz Book

A perennial favourite, this small book contains a number of sections of graded questions that will allow one to test their Bible knowledge or to be used in a setting where others are quizzed on their depth of Bible knowledge and trivia.

Missing at Calvary

A book filled with meditations on Calvary eminently suitable for the Easter season. Mr Davies writes concerning a number of things which will not be found at Calvary and uses this vehicle to lead the reader into holy places where the remarkable story of God's love is clearly demonstrated in his clear choice of stories.

Your Path to Health (not yet published)

This book is in process of being completed for publication. In it, Mr Davies draws on his 90-plus years of living and personal experience during those years to present to the reader numerous anecdotes and sage advice on food, exercise, and many other ingredients that foster wellness – drawn essentially from a Scriptural basis.

These publications may be ordered from:

The Christian Book Shop
P O Box N-4924
Nassau, Bahamas

Telephone (242) 322-1306

Or

The Miracle Prayer Fellowship
P O Box DO 1022
Cardiff
South Wales,
United Kingdom